THEME OF LINE

Chuck Joy

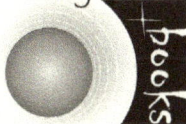

red giant books

Theme of Line

Red Giant Books

ISBN: 978-0-9968717-6-1

10 9 8 7 6 5 4 3 2 1

Printed in the United States of America.

www.redgiantbooks.com

for Rob

Line

FIRST LINES

a first line
is still a line,
first line presents itself, sings, jumps, bangs a drum
does all the things lines do,
first lines just do it first

first lines open
they wait all day to take the stage
approach the podium, clear their throats
then carry us away,
they launch

first lines bridge the gap
between the near shore, green with summer
short docks poked from every narrow cottage
and the north rim, black with forest
horsey creatures snorting through a mist

first lines must be comfortable
in their own skin, the other lines
count on them, follow them, models
their sashays down the catwalk
all variations on that first theme

meandering vowels twist oxbows
through the valley of the line
consonants, chittering, rain hail
hail on the gray roof of a tin shed,

such a thunderstorm

first lines melt the clouds away
shine the sun again, make it summer
first lines send us on vacation
they wish us bon voyage, bonne chance
last lines welcome us back

LOST LINE

life is suffering, little Buddha
illusion then it's gone

the last poem, composed
transcribed, filed to the computer, posted
printed, published, read from a stage
(in fact, in Cleveland)

life, the suffering inside my picture window
outside too, vehicles and people
some of them people I know
yes, it's remarkable how far I can go
how many episodes, among strangers
everybody talking, friends and strangers
talking or preparing to talk

up in here, the bridge behind my eyes
the bridge where I am captain and crew
the voice that never stills controls the intercom
constantly messaging, sometimes a klaxon horn
sometimes music but really words
words in lines, one at a time
assembled to various lengths

amid the words, all these words
within and without, at a very rare frequency
certain words strike a spark
a tiny flash but of such great intensity

their fire can burn for awhile
providing the light and heat without which all is cold and dark

my job is to catch a spark
then nurture it through an entire burn
I have learned a series of techniques, over the many years
to recognize and capture them, the sparks
a discipline, like breathing

I patrol this field, a shortstop
my ears my glove, my imagination
the crowd attentive to my efforts
rewarding every catch with at least polite applause
unless I miss, and then there isn't any compensation
if I don't catch the spark, that spark is gone and gone forever
lost line

A LINE OF POETRY

what makes a line of poetry
for me rarely includes a joke

not like some poets
some poets can crack you up
from beginning to end
funny poets
they could be comedians

I can be funny
I write fun poetry
but lines for me are just hot
their curves burning from the page
splashed with special powder, flickering color
where's the joke?

lines aim for awesomeness
as do we all, invoking that altered state of consciousness
delight, where anything can happen
the imagination! at the junction of theatre and music
listen: I bathe in the waters of love or
now we are in Ancient Rome, wait
it's only a plastic model!

lines fill our ears
with sustenance, timelessness
now we are smaller than atoms
wandering about inside the nucleus, a fabulous gallery

distinguishing protons from neutrons

lines induce peace
a trance, an exit from the body
yet alert to every nearby particular
a spluttering candle, the creak of floorboards

lines so sweet they ease you to sleep
dream your own dream

HOME ALONE LINES

1.
untying knots from thoughts
pulling ropes with both hands

extraterrestrials mistaking dogs for the crown of earthly
    creation
dogs I tell ya

the voice speaks its own cadence
determines stanza length itself

indulge your inner lesbian
position by position

if we're from anywhere other than Pennsylvania
it's New York!

avuncular, jocular, celtic-themed
thank you Billy Collins

nothing like rain in deep city
helps you accept the lines you forgot

rain dripping from the lip of the marquee
round white lightbulbs, tall gray buildings

Jayne Mansfield with you
wearing her heart on her sleeve

what is truth?
what is form?

2.
the blues is a groove, man
with pattern to the lyrics, a rhyme scheme
my baby went to New York City
left me here home alone
my baby went to New York City
she left me here all alone at home
the bed, I think it's broken
the AM radio is always on

am I so easily amused?
a tailor cutting pants too short?
my imagination a cowed dog?
growling dog my foot
titles are a line
they're all lines
theme of line

TWO

ABSOLUTELY PRESENT

I've done enough exactly backwards
to find myself exactly where we are

a bloodless chain of lovely words
you read or better yet, hear being read

their subtle music, simply thought
recorded from an inner voice, still hot

inscribed against the marble of experience
just so, chips littering the silent studio

*   *   *

outside, blue sky fills with cloud
snow falls thick this far north

dark figures, helicopters
wherein we await, already passengers

a radio crackles with news from the front
soon we are carried to a great city

broad avenues, bright with light
closer in, coffee bars, jazz clubs

my friend knows the one for us
we file in, attractive, troubled

*   *   *

Poetry Night at the Be Here Now Café
Buster Miracle, featured poet

here's a poet with a cute gimmick
something from nothing, right onstage

his entire existence, this very appearance
no bio, no credits, no parents

or children or colleagues or main squeeze
no relationships at all, nothing

just this performance, brief like fire
absolutely present yes, that's it

RASCAL NEW YORK
A Comedy

1. Arrival

In the spirit of Laura Nyro
   Charles Bukowski and August Wilson
I, Denzel Washington, approached the great city.

City of my fondest hopes
   my worst despair
most grandiose, most wretched
     which had I never left
     I would never have met you.

Now I'm on my way to Broadway
   yet again, to play the rascal poet
Ratko Basic
   a Serbian villain
in the second of three one-act plays
composed by my Italian-American friend
   Benito Colavito
     I owed him a favor.

I had intended to review the script
   on the way but
the silver beauty of the Hudson Valley
   attracted me, the window
     of the train a screen.
My kind of movie!

The King Lear, my hotel
muy convenient to the subway and then dinner
with Coulehan at Airoso although, on the way
            I experienced hallucination
               when I was sure I saw us together, you and me
        standing in the 51st Street station, Lexington Avenue line
              the uptown express smashing past.
I knew to be very careful.

After dinner, alone, I wandered happily homeward
home, for the next three days at least
        The King Lear, Eighth and Forty-fifth
        side-stepping the sidewalk crowd
        identifying their various languages

2. The Show

Practice went badly, my partner
Cordelia, too shy to speak.

To soothe myself, I fell in
with a baseball game, fourteen year-olds
        playing in a park on the Far West Side
we could see New Jersey
            from the outfield
and I realized I had never given up.

I *had* searched Poetry Monday Hell's Kitchen
        confident and found
two women one younger the other

in a sea green shirt with a sky
        dark scarf, reciting
their lines on a third floor
for an audience of twelve including me, Denzel.

        The next day after practice
        Colavito insisted
us having dinner on Mulberry Street.
We both had tortellini alla panna
        white sauce prosciutto and mushrooms and peas
then walked almost all the way across
        Manhattan in the rain to join his son
                the quote poet
supposedly reading on MacDougall
        or Cornelia Street.

        Tuesday night our show, well-received.
I was pleased with my performance
the experience uplifting.
        Cordelia might have been
        playing with me,
                she really needed no practice.

3. Denzel

I love this work
        doing these jobs.
Ratko a challenge, the poet part
easy but he was also a psychiatrist.
        I think I played him as a pediatrician,

Serbians have children, little Ratko
    loved Sarajevo, I betcha.

I love poetry, remember
the Howdy Spring Poetry Festival
at City College?
    George Dickerson reading
    his memorial to Thomas M. Catterson?
Diane Wakoski in attendance
gracious as ever.

    Ratko's a character
    an opportunity.
Me, I would never eat at Neptune
    (Polish place on First Avenue)
an open-fronted bar,
a yellow green and strawberry-painted
    vegetarian restaurant across the street
then boogie south to Church, talking to myself
    enter a semi-finished white room
        short rows of folding chairs
    adults, women and men
black-haired most of them
reading poems
reciting them
their own or about love
    a puzzled dove waiting stunned
        uncertain breathing without you
            strutting the blues to the radio
                by Pablo Neruda
okay maybe I would.

4. Tendaberry

Yesterday I awoke to the radio
playing Laura Nyro, her death
         one of many blows to this great city
changed a fifty, bought seven postage stamps
ate breakfast at a breakfast place behind Port Authority
         scrambled eggs, crisp bacon
         tomato juice small, rye toast
enjoyed a paper cup of good strong coffee
met Mary Beth for a condensed visit to the Whitney Museum
         returned to The King Lear
                  and checked out.

PROJECTIVE RECOGNITION

misidentifying strangers
as people you know

often occurs while travelling

the dude three chairs down the beach
could be that kid from high school
what's his name? Dennis?
or the girl at the coffee cart
could be your cousin Amy

except she isn't Amy
and he isn't Dennis

if you're not otherwise busy
you can spend productive time
remembering Amy or Dennis
and why you might want to see them

projective recognition

THE ANXIETY

I meet you
at the first tee, the end of a long tunnel
tighter and darker the farther I push myself,
conversation slowing among the others
in the gallery, watching

watching us, me and you, my friend
you, jumping around in your ludicrous clownsuit
the ruffled sleeves, the polka dots, the bells
bells at the ends of the leaves of that floppy hat

attached to the shaft of a hefty driver
that's me, hanging on for dear life
me, rather anywhere other than here
this pock-marked hillock
splintered tees, red and yellow
littering the haggard ground

oh we're a pair
me in my blue shorts, my green golf-shirt
forgetting all about the present moment
the juicy confidence of a grooved swing
a simple play within yourself
all that's really necessary

instead, I get the scoundrel
you, prancing the tee like a stage

all cartwheels and honks

making a big ridiculous production

of a summer afternoon

THE 24/7

forever on stage
thinking in lines
even sleeping rarely alone

you know you can post when
you can invoke the experience of actual speech
right down to the neurotic features,

the appearances, at book stores, art museums
parts in ensemble documentaries
the appearances are samples
samples from the 24/7, dig?

certain sequences are animated
you should see these animated sequences live!
when the animation coincides with an appearance, it's the
    bomb
happy strangers eagerly turning their dollars into books
later never quite sure their book isn't still animated
even on a bedside table, they were reading from the book to
    their gumar
a busty babe with lots of cabernet black hair
complaining the English was making her ears hurt

especially at moments of intimacy and nakedness
or while public speaking
addressing a crowd such as yourselves
my friends, our few minutes together

the poetry samples the poetry
like Neil Young never said, It's all one poem
you can take some home

when we're together like we are now
the present moment is fulfilled in our togetherness

CARTOON LIFE

the animated world
cartoon life
a little car, bright red, all curving fenders
squeals through a corner for a hard left turn
tires whirling, puffs of smoke
pulls back, as if to launch itself
then shoots away, out of the frame

inside that car, a cartoon hand
three fingers and a thumb
paws at the dashboard, pushing buttons for the radio
an angry voice, reading news
push, a woman's voice, talking about football
push, ukulele music
purple quarter-notes pour from the speakers

the cartoon car bounces to a stop
at a curb, outside a looming storefront
all soft ledges and curtained windows

a woman appears on the sidewalk
a cartoon woman in a long coat with a fur collar
holding a poodle, she speaks
her voice like a klaxon horn
with a lisp,
Thimon! We've been mithing you!

the car's door popped open
Simon emerging from the driver's seat

a lizard, green, a tall lizard, our Simon
wearing a white shirt
and a toothy smile

it's always warm in cartoon land
or cold, heat-waves rising from spaceheaters

I DIED IN BOSTON

I died in Boston
at the station, waiting for the train to take me home

an iron fixture, rusted through
detached from the high roof
smashed me flat against platform seven
I never saw it coming

I was there
then I was gone

one young man (we had exchanged two lines
the train, it's late? yes, several minutes)
stared at the fallen me, the smile he had raised
left hanging on his face

had the train been on time
I would still be alive

a pretty coed dropped her books
one book bounced toward my left foot
(oddly twisted, that foot
to an angle unavailable in life)
if she considered screaming, making a big scene
throwing herself to the floor or just her cellphone
she didn't show it

an unintended community
gathered around the dead me

one lovely woman
her lips twisted, her black sweater tight
(might my last thought have been about her breasts?)
a new friend, we had traded brief bios, me about me
she a singer-songwriter

vivid with grief (appropriate to the length of our relationship
exactly seventeen minutes)
her sobs stopped short when the train did come

she boarded, finding a seat
next to another handsome prince

DREAMY

ABOUT MY LIFE (ALL POETRY)

I admire serious people
like Matt, when we burned that rubber trash
Matt was really upset about the unchecked acrid smoke
me, I'd leave it alone

here's the thing, about my life
I have been fortunate, I like my work
I love my wife, you guys are cool
it's been a great ride
I look forward to the future
because when it comes to death
when it comes to death
it's all about poetry, all poetry

MEDICAL POETRY
LEGAL IN CALIFORNIA

also in New Jersey, they say
where a doctor has the opportunity
to make poetry available,
will insurance pay?

poetry, a powerful and nonspecific
consciousness enhancer
known for millennia, recognized
throughout the Muslim and the Hindu world
more recently come to America,
popular with jazz musicians

now with medicinal properties
a group of therapists including physicians
I among them, believed to ease the pain of death
to treat persistent illness,
perhaps especially when traditional
Western methods are hopeless

not without side effects, poetry
might exacerbate psychosis
affective or otherwise; users
can become preoccupied, obsessed
with its benefits, their lives
empty without poetry present

medical poetry, every detail
not entirely worked out yet,
the best dose, the length of the treatment
a social experiment, health science

FASTEN YOUR SEATBELT

some behaviors are so extreme
they need their own language
get likkered up
shoot out the lights

another good reason not to own a gun
because you might, one night
abruptly decide to give up not drinking
having left your fucking wife
alone in the big house long enough

that's right
give me another of those Canadian whiskies
I like Canadian whiskey, I should drink it more often

drive up Highway Sixty, fast
your world a black tunnel
white lines flashing, yellow lights
turn up the music, try not to be sick

jump out the truck in the driveway
head for the bedroom, where the gun is
the fucking wife meets you halfway up the stairs
all flowing blue nightgown and white robe
soon she is screaming like a wounded child
pushed past you to the kitchen and the telephone

upstairs find the gun but don't
remember shooting the windows out, one by one by one

or plugging both pillows, right through their centers
or shooting the television and the computer

the SWAT Team, the tear gas, the being brought down
the wife pursuing mental health procedures
emergency vehicles parked every which way
red light splashing the commitment papers

wake up in the hospital, still a bear
but ready to go, I'm not staying here
meet the psychiatrist, you're not going anywhere
for five days sir, his voice quavering
distant, polite, you wish you could shoot him too

LINES WRITTEN FROM SLEEP

you can't blow over a house of bricks
try it, if the house falls
something is really wrong

DAYS, TWO

1.
one day I decided my poetry persona needed more Mick Jagger
it was a Wednesday

I would purse my lips
hike back my elbows
and strut

the universal voice of poetry
speaking through me

every line straight to thin air

2.
another day I felt the reality of blackness
a reliable presence
enters through the radio if not your skin

the page steadies me
so many lines
waiting for a place to happen
making stops along the way

WORDS AT THE EDGE

all this talking to myself
mumbling numbers writing a check, thirty seven dollars and
    zero zero cents
obsessing song lyrics, *you're not the ocean*
some observations so crisp
they go straight to Twitter

rare stretches of arid consciousness
empty highway, desert
window open, Sirius competing with the rush of hot air
me behind the wheel weighing risks and benefits
"which" or "that"

music, slap of sticks to drum
bass comes in, bumpy hum
a guy from high school strums a guitar
fingering strings, digging deep
let's talk about poetry

some lines grabbed from the radio
or studied on lyric sheets, am I right?
one point, maybe not *the* point, but *a* point
one big point for me is to gab my lines with that same intensity
words at the edge of singing
a band playing in my head

now the band plays in your head too, listen to the silence
yes that's a saxophone blowing and blowing
long choruses, flashy cadences of notes
James Baldwin heard it best, Love me, love *me*

NEIL YOUNG

Buffalo Springfield, big in '67, 1968. Neil Young in Los Angeles. Imagine he'd been all around Canada by then. From Winnipeg. Then Toronto, where they have the Farmer's Market. I like that about him, Neil Young. The Canada part. I'm not sure how I feel about the Los Angeles.

Yet there we were in New York. New York, New York, borough of the Bronx, a flat on Webster Avenue, behind a red and black Edward Hopper façade. Those were the days. Old Man and Cinnamon Girl. Times were troubled. Some of us entered medical school. Neil Young made a movie, and kept making records. *On The Beach. Tonight's The Night.*

I watched the movie in The Kings Court, Pittsburgh, Oakland Pittsburgh, from plush black-and-yellow seats much worse for the wear. I remember dark shapes on the screen, and horses. Years later, in San Francisco, on Haight Street, Amoeba Records, I buy the vinyl *Time Fades Away* in a cellophane envelope, carry it home on the airplane. I'm listening to it now.

Neil Young's music, roots like a thick tree, down by the river, where it meets the blues, European music including French, western swing, then rock and roll (there's the big news) even country. Best place to hear Neil Young on Sirius XM is Outlaw Country. Rocking that sweet spot, often with Crazy Horse. Singer, songwriter, bandleader, director, sometimes he seems edgy. Who imagined a world of such success, and grandchildren? *Mirror Ball. Chrome Dreams II.*

We caught him in Morgantown, West Virginia, the basketball pavilion filled with gunslingers and second-shift nurses, concerned citizens, well-scrubbed Mountaineers, their professors, veterans, unemployed coalminers. Neil Young was either part of or with The Shocking Pinks. Could there have been a more unfortunate period in which to catch Neil Young? An homage to a formative cultural period just before my own. Maybe *Trans*, one or two cultural periods later. Meanwhile my little sister gets to see *Rust Never Sleeps*.

He's a model for me, Neil Young, creativity through the life cycle. I try poetry and what I call poetry values lyrics including Neil Young's. Even his handwriting an inspiration to me, the way he prints, the same way as my dad's cursive. My wife, her mother, our daughter, her husband, we watched *Greendale* two floors above Old Harbor Street, South Boston, an ocean beach at the end of Old Harbor Street, Carson Beach, the Atlantic Ocean.

Don't let it bring you down it's only castles burning. When I was low, turning those big wheels in the tobacco factory and again, driving west across Interstate 8, on my way to Iowa City, ready to test my chops as best I could. *Psychedelic Pill. Zuma.* He's been a big influence. *Neil Young.*

SPACE TRAVEL

observe the earth, planet Earth, from space
far enough away to recognize
our insignificance

now focus closer
identify the wealth of blue
the familiar outlines of landmass
be patient for the clouds to clear
seek North America

approach from the Atlantic Coast
avoid New York, you could fall in there and never come out
those narrow streets between tenement walkups
their fire escapes, their jumble of signs
a permanent crowd overfilling the sidewalk
everything black-and-white

find the lakes, the Great Lakes
a water feature notable for the entire globe
see Chicago?
hear that elevated train banging past black-brick buildings
guys on the corner, black-and-red flannel jackets
their hands in their pockets?
women in headscarves, pushing strollers?
you've gone too far
pull back

here's Toronto
see the lakefront development

the forest of condos, the Tower?
further north it's the poetry neighborhood
big book stores, multiple floors well-lit behind glass front walls
cool cafeterias, serving meatloaf and French food
steam trays to wooden tables, everybody wearing sweaters

several venues poetry is featured
backrooms of restaurants or music clubs
long bars, rows of tables with red chairs
one stage on a second floor,
I'll get off here

DREAMY

Rick lifted his lips
from Donnajean's lips
his tongue from her tongue

they were in the bedroom
of his trailer, outside
bright stars, a crescent moon

black sky, the far plateau
white in the night shine
the broad valley
divided by a coiled wash
braids of water silver
cottonwoods here and there

inside, a window, faux pine wall
a wide poster (Georgia O'Keeffe *Green Mesa*)
a desk, a chair, a dresser
littered with their clothes

Donnajean on her back
across the bed, her hair
blonde and red, spread
behind her head, blues music
playing from a CD deck

Rick adjusted
his thrusting and gasped How's that
Donnajean snapped her arms behind his back

pushed up at him with the same rhythm, laughed
answered Dreamy

THEME

POWER LINES

lines appear, short lines
pairs and threes
arranged across a page, a stiff page
formal like an invitation
uneven, many lines less long
content lost, shape remaining

now we're in modern Florence
Firenze, il Duomo, inside
a service about to take place
your boss in a black dress
everyone wearing black hoods
sorting themselves into ranks
it's a funeral, organ music rising
you wish you were somewhere else

like at lunch, on a patio
vines and trellis overhead
sharing a square table
white tablecloth, elegant silverware
goblets half-filled with wine like red velvet
a black-vested waiter delivering shallow plates
spaghettini amatriciana
shaved cheese?

the weather changing for the better
a fat gray canopy of cloud retreating to the east
revealing blue sky and soon sun

BEAUTIFULS

learning to be neutral
learning to be still, simply
occupying space,
that's beautiful

a holiday spirit
accelerating gently, daily
many weeks, until it peaks
cresting steadily, then ebbing
settling yet maintaining
that's beautiful

a line of words
carrying imagination down the page
yours, your voice to speak the words
they speak, their stories
their music, they're friends!
that's beautiful

BETWEEN THE LINES

between the lines
are spaces
they're the best!

I hear music
often, in those silences
original compositions
short pieces, sound effects
train whistles

sometimes stage directions
gesture, with gun
step forward, smile

an editor works in there
his office high above Manhattan
that last line, he wonders
maybe change the location
and why is everybody laughing

various observers
surface, a regular circus
some children shouting their comments
others too nervous to speak, young men
checking out the girls in the audience,
old guys eyeing their spouses,
somebody's parents

one voice speaks, the voice
the poetry voice, the whole point
this voice

that voice silent, you can't hear it
me, I prefer imagining
the cup of voice half-filled

WE STAND ON THE SHOULDERS OF GIANTS

slot the words into a proper order
every line with its own personality
some lines especially stunning or spilling over
to the next line, a little surprise but all the lines
measured, drumming their little songs

the presence of an alphabet supports the hypothesis
civilization precedes our consciousness

Chuck Joy

Both his parents from western New York, and carried by them to Erie Pennsylvania in the first year of life, Chuck considers his birth in Cleveland Ohio an "accident". He has since lived away from Erie for extended periods, usually for educational reasons, visiting New York City, Pittsburgh Pennsylvania, Warren Pennsylvania, northern New Mexico, Portland Oregon, and Morgantown West Virginia. In Portland, around 1979, Chuck started writing, early publications in Bogg and Medicinal Purposes, early appearances in Meadville PA and at the Orange Bear. Joy's poems have appeared in Crisis Chronicles, Psychopoetica, Rattapallax, Tobeco, Great Lakes Review, Guide to Kulchur, and 2 Bridges, and have been included in anthologies edited by John Graham-Pole, Berwyn Moore, Jack Coulehan, and Sean Thomas Dougherty. He has appeared as featured poet at Woodlawn Diner in Buffalo and Mahall's 20 Lanes in Cleveland, the Confluence festival in Pittsburgh, Saturn Series, the Cornelia Street Café, and every Snoetry. Nickname of "C. Boogie", Chuck contributes regularly at Poets' Hall in Erie. He co-created and hosted Poetry Scene at the Erie Book Store, a weekly poetry event with open mic and featured poets, for eight years. Chuck Joy is a member of the Italian American Writers Association, and the Second Tuesday poetry workshop at Mercyhurst University. A community child psychiatrist, Dr. Chuck is the co-chair of their Art Committee. The poems selected for this collection, Theme Of Line, focus around style. Previous collections include Fun Poetry (lulu.com), All Smooth (Destitute Press, Buffalo NY), Every Tiger Wants To Sing (Poets' Hall Press, Erie PA), and Said the Growling Dog (Nirala Publications, New Delhi, India). Chuck lives with his wife Dawn. More at chuckjoy.com.

www.ingramcontent.com/pod-product-compliance
Lightning Source LLC
Chambersburg PA
CBHW031342040426
42443CB00006B/450